The College Panda

ACT Essay

The Battle-tested Guide for ACT Writing

ISBN: 978-0-9894964-5-2

For more information, visit thecollegepanda.com

Discounts available for teachers and companies. Please contact thecollegepanda@gmail.com for details.

Table of Contents

Trying to Hit a Moving Target

In 2015, the ACT announced significant changes to the test that would take effect in September. Among these changes were a dual reading passage and tougher English grammar questions, but the only section that was completely rehauled was the essay.

Previously, you had 30 minutes to take a position on an issue such as *Should 20% of television programming be devoted to educational shows?* Now, you're given 40 minutes to write something much more complicated. Not only must you take a position on an issue, but you also must consider 3 given perspectives and weave a discussion of them into your essay. An example prompt would look something like this:

Safety and Privacy

In an age when technology and social media allow others to peer more deeply into our lives than ever before, the conflict between the right to privacy and the need for safety has intensified. For example, government surveillance captures our text messages and phone calls in order to obtain information to thwart terrorist attacks. Security cameras in school deter and solve crime but may not promote a comfortable environment for students to express themselves. What is lost when we limit privacy for security and what is gained? Given the constantly changing dynamic between privacy and safety in our digital world, it is worth considering whether one should be sacrificed for the other.

Read and consider these perspectives. Each suggests a particular way of thinking about the conflict between safety and privacy.

Perspective One	Perspective Two	Perspective Three
Government cannot keep us safe without relevant information. Privacy must sometimes be given up so that law enforcement has the resources necessary to protect us.	Privacy should be limited so that we live in a more transparent society. An increased awareness of those around us helps us make safer decisions.	What could keep society more safe than privacy itself? When personal information can easily be obtained, public safety is compromised.

Essay Task

Write a unified, coherent essay in which you evaluate multiple perspectives on the conflict between safety and privacy. In your essay, be sure to:

- analyze and evaluate the perspectives given
- state and develop your own perspective on the issue
- explain the relationship between your perspective and those given

Your perspective may be in full agreement with any of the others, in partial agreement, or wholly different. Whatever the case, support your ideas with logical reasoning and detailed, persuasive examples.

Once your essay is sent in, two readers each give it a score from 1-6 in four categories: Ideas and Analysis, Development and Support, Organization, Language Use and Conventions. The scores for each category are summed up to get the category's Domain Score.

	1st Reader 1-6		2nd Reader 1-6		Domain Score 2-12
Ideas and Analysis	_____	+	_____	=	_____
Development and Support	_____	+	_____	=	_____
Organization	_____	+	_____	=	_____
Language Use and Conventions	_____	+	_____	=	_____

The four Domain Scores are then added up to get the Raw Score, a value between 8 and 48. Finally, the Raw Score is translated to a Scaled Score on the basis of a curve, which likely changes from test to test. This Scaled Score is your final writing score; it's what colleges look at. The following tables show the curve from the December 2015 exam.

Raw Score	Scaled Score
48	36
—	35
—	34
47	33
46	32
45	31
44	30
42-43	29
41	28
40	27
39	26
38	25
36-37	24
33-35	23
32	22
31	21
29-30	20
28	19

Raw Score	Scaled Score
27	18
25-26	17
24	16
23	15
22	14
21	13
19-20	12
18	11
17	10
16	9
15	8
14	7
13	6
12	5
11	4
10	3
—	2
8-9	1

As you can see, the writing score goes from 1 (worst) to 36 (best), the same point scale used for all the other sections on the ACT. Note that the writing score is now separate from the English section score and does not factor into the overall ACT composite score.

Since the update was announced, the grading of the updated essay format has become quite the black box of mystery. The ACT's vague and useless grading rubric certainly hasn't helped matters. Not only are teachers and students struggling to figure out what's expected on the essay, but the ACT graders themselves don't seem to know how to grade the responses.

Throughout 2015 and early 2016, after the new essay had been put in place, the ACT took much longer than usual in releasing writing scores. In fact, the delays put many students' early action and early decision applications in jeopardy. And when scores were finally released, some students who received high scores on the English section received strangely low scores on the essay. This disparity led many to question the ACT's new grading practices. Angry students who requested their test be hand-scored experienced as much as 15 point gains (from 21 to 36) after their essays were regraded. Many colleges, aware of the issues plaguing the ACT, weighed the essay less heavily in 2015 or removed it from consideration altogether.

As it turns out, the ACT was making serious grading errors on the essay section. Grading standards weren't consistent across all graders. Some scores were switched with others. The whole mess only added to the controversy over the new changes, which many felt were not communicated well enough to the first test-takers in early 2015.

At this point, it looks like the ACT has resolved its problems, but our problem still remains—how do we approach an essay that until recently has been a moving target, especially when no one has had enough experience with it to see what works and what doesn't?

That's the problem this book aims to solve, and it does so by offering a battle-tested essay template that I've used personally on an actual administration of the exam to get a perfect 36.

But before we get to the template, let's first learn as much as we can about what the ACT is actually looking for.

My Experiment to Find What the ACT Graders Want

Even though I am well out of college, I found the ACT essay to be such an unknown that for the sake of my students, I decided to take the ACT myself. My plan was to take it in December of 2015 and February of 2016, tweaking my essay in specific ways each time to see how the graders would respond.

The goal wasn't to get a perfect score just to brag that I could do it. Nor was it to show you fancy essays that only I could write. **The goal was to develop a framework for the perfect essay that could be replicated by all students and applied to all prompts.**

So off I went.

Before my first test date in December, I read everything I could to get a basic idea of what a great ACT essay might look like. The only official resources available were 2 sample prompts released by the ACT and a few sample student essays. Nothing was particularly insightful or definitive enough to give me all the answers but I did glean something very important when I read the high-scoring sample essays: **Don't refer to the perspectives by their number.**

The following is a screenshot of the top-scoring (6 in all categories) sample essay on the ACT website when the essay changes first took effect in September 2015.

Sample Essay 6

Ideas and Analysis: Score = 6
Development and Support: Score = 6
Organization: Score = 6
Language Use and Conventions: Score = 6

Begin WRITING TEST Here.

As technology improves, and more and more tasks are completed by machines instead of humans. the question is no longer about what we can do with machines, but rather what we should. Although the usage of machines increases efficiency and our standard of living, it detracts from the value of human life.

As machines increasingly perform all our basic tasks, society is able to produce more. The additional production adds material value to our society and frees people up from these low-skill tasks. This is in agreement with Perspective Two which claims that this industrialization leads to more prosperity. For example, in the 18th century, short-staple cotton that was grown in the Southern United States required an immense amount of labor in order to seperate the seeds from the fiber to process the cotton to make it marketable. However, in the mid-19th century, Eli Whitney, an American entrepreneur, invented the cotton gin, which allowed for automation of cotton processing. This machine replaced the need of a large work force for the process and greatly improved production. As a result of the cotton gin, short-staple cotton production skyrocketed, increasing by more than 10 times in the South while bringing prosperity to the region and setting in motion a new industrial era in America. This is in agreement with Perspective Three. which says that mechanization allows for "unimagined possibilities". Although there are clearly many advantages to industrialization, there are also some heavy drawbacks.

The replacement of humans by machines leads to the loss of value to human life. an effect that outweighs the material gains of automation. The search to find human tasks that can be performed by machines inevitably leads to comparisons between the human and the machine. If a company executive wants to see if a inventory management team can be replaced by a robotic system, he will compare the two and determine which can do a better job. When this occurs, the people on the team are evaluated not for their worth as human beings, but for their effectiveness at performing a specific function — in essence, as we would evaluate a machine. In a larger sense, when we begin to think about humans in this way, the worth of a person's life becomes dependent on only what they can do and no longer has any intrinsic value. As Perspective One states, we begin to lose our humanity. This new mindset and way of evaluating people, though seemingly harmless in the workplace, is devastating when it begins to pervade a society. If a person is judged only on his or her capability, there is no reason for a person to remain after they have served their function. This would warrant genocide against the elderly and the disabled because their burden on society would not be made up for by any production. Although the machines may seem to only fulfill the low skill jobs at the moment, there is no barrier to prevent the machines from replacing more. As the machines increase in intelligence, they will replace any tasks done by humans and render us unnecessary and worthless.

Due to the risks of dehumanization, the material benefits of machines are not enough to justify its increasing presence.

Notice that the writer refers to the three perspectives as Perspective One, Two, and Three, as highlighted. But as the months went by and the ACT continued to refine the new essay and its grading practices in the face of its grading controversy, it became clear that things had changed. The previous top-scoring sample essay was taken down and the following one was put in its place.

Sample Essay 6

Ideas and Analysis: Score = 6
Development and Support: Score = 6
Organization: Score = 6
Language Use and Conventions: Score = 6

Begin WRITING TEST Here.

Advances in technology have become so widely accepted in today's culture that very few people are willing to pause to consider the consequences. People get so excited about what new technologies can offer that they forget to question whether there might be any negative effects. Without caution and deliberation, replacing the natural with the mechanical would undoubtedly be disasterous.

The economic implications of the potential mechanical takeover alone should be enough to dissuade anyone from moving too fast. In the event the robots are more widely used in the workplace, humans would surely be replaced. At first, businesses would benefit from the efficiency of robots, but eventually a depressed job market would lead to a population that struggles just to feed themselves and their families, let alone purchase the products these robots make. In the long run, society will suffer if it does not take care to prevent the economic consequences of giving everything over to machines.

Our careless use of automation has already taken a toll on our culture. People have been interacting with automation in nearly every aspect of their lives, whether it be shopping, banking, or the use of a telephone. The effect of this is obvious: basic respect for our fellow man is all but absent today because of increased interaction with automation. Why treat a machine with kindness? It suffers no emotional or psychological damage. In a culture saturated with automation, we get used to treating machines rudely, and we begin to treat each other rudely. This of course leads to all sorts of issues, like intolerance and incivility, and in the long run, results in the complete degradation of culture.

Even in the face of these obstacles, some people argue that the increasing intelligence of today's machines is a good thing. After all, machine power can decrease the human work load. Computer processers double in power and ability every year. Computers are projected to reach human intelligence by as soon as 2025. The implications of this shift are unknown, but one thing is for certain. We are moving into this change too fast to anticipate and prevent damage to the human species. We are approaching this change too quickly for any sort of safety net to be built. Because of this, it is important that we as a species slow down our technological development so that we might consider all the implications of a change this big. We must figure out how to handle negative societal and cultural consequences before we embrace total integration of automated, intelligent machines.

Decreasing the speed with which we incorporate mechanical influence is important because of the potential dangers that lurk in blind acceptance. Not only does the preference of the mechanical over the natural interfere with the job market and the economy, but its use also has the potential to seriously degrade our culture as a whole. In combination with the uncertainty surrounding the increasing intelligence of machines, it is most assuredly better for the human species that technological progress be slowed so that we can, if necessary, prevent additional damage.

At the time of this book's publication, this essay is still the model essay on the site. As you can see, there are no references to Perspective One, Two, or Three. The writer weaves the various viewpoints into the essay without mentioning them explicitly.

Given these developments, it's fair to assume that it's not ideal to refer to the perspectives by their number. This is not to say that you can't get a perfect score if you do, but the fact that the ACT took the effort to change their model essay is a clear sign the graders prefer that you don't.

With this one piece of the puzzle solved, I was able to cobble together a simple template that I would use as an experiment to help me uncover other characteristics of a perfect essay.

As it turns out, the first time's the charm because I managed to get a perfect 36 using that template, which I will share with you later in this book.

Because the template worked out so well, I was able to experiment a bit more the second time to see whether certain factors would hurt me or keep me at a perfect score. I kept some components of the template the same but altered other characteristics of the essay, such as the length and my example types.

The results were still good—a score of 32—but it was clear my experimental changes didn't help. Still, this gave me added confidence in my template.

So what exactly did I tweak from the first essay to the second?

The first thing was the length. My second essay was about a third of a page shorter than my first one. I didn't intentionally write a shorter essay the second time around; it just turned out that way.

The second thing was using logic in place of examples. In my first essay, I discussed apps such as AirBnB and websites such as Amazon to support my argument. **These were examples that I had prepared and perfected beforehand.** In my second essay, I didn't discuss as many specific examples, relying on logic instead. To illustrate what this means, imagine that you're writing an essay that argues against monopolies.

If you were supporting your argument with examples, you might talk about how Theodore Roosevelt broke up the Standard Oil and American Sugar companies to encourage competition in 1905, or how the recklessness of big banks led to the financial crisis of 2008. But if you were supporting your argument with logic, you might instead talk about how monopolies hurt the consumers and lead to inefficiencies and a lack of innovation. See the difference? Essays that are based on logic are more general and theoretical.

It's not that essays based on pure logic are bad. In fact, the ACT's top sample essays are logic-based ones. It's just that the example-based approach allows for more preparation and requires less on-the-fly thinking during the exam. It's less prone to writer's block. Ideally, you want as much of your essay to be stuff you've rehearsed before rather than stuff you're making up on the spot. If you end up getting a tough prompt that nullifies your preparation, you can always resort to a logic-based argument as a fallback.

So the problem with my second essay wasn't that it was logic-based, but that the logic wasn't being expressed in a well-thought-out and organized manner in the heat of time pressure. Like I said, it's tough to improvise.

As we'll see, my preferred approach uses a combination of both examples and logic, but it's the examples that take center stage.

In the next chapter, I'll give you a general summary of my experiments by laying out the essential elements of a perfect essay. In the following chapters, I'll show you the template I used as well as the exact ACT essay that received a perfect score. I was able to retrieve this essay through the ACT's Test Information Release service, which is offered in December, April, and June. Unfortunately, it's not offered in February so I wasn't able to get a copy of my second essay, but the takeaways from that experience, some of which we've just discussed, will no doubt be described throughout this book.

The 6 Elements of a Perfect Essay

Despite the ACT's past inconsistencies, the grading process is extremely standardized to ensure that scores remain consistent across the board. Graders are given a checklist of things to look for, and they're trained to put their own opinions aside and base their scores solely on the models that have already been set. And given the sheer number of essays that must be read, they're required to be quick.

As a result, they won't spend any longer than TWO MINUTES reading your paper. Two minutes and that's it. It's a snap judgment: *Does this essay look like a 6? Yep. Next!* Any flashes of your literary brilliance will be glossed over in a ruthless grading procedure that only cares about whether your work matches the standard model.

Your job, then, is not to write a masterpiece. This isn't AP English. The teacher won't be looking at every word and dissecting every little thing you did wrong.

Instead, your job is simply to write something that looks like a 6. Write something that looks smart, something that looks like all the essays that have been awarded 6's before, and you in turn will be rewarded with a final score of 36. That's it. It doesn't have to be innovative and it doesn't have to be in your voice and style. Just give them what they want.

Whenever I explain this mindset to students, there's always a slight outcry because it conflicts with the creative writing process they've been taught throughout school. A lot of students want to stand behind their own writing abilities instead of relying on any kind of pre-scripted formula. "I'm already a good writer," they say. "I don't need to follow a template."

I totally understand. As much as I would like the essay portion to be less of a game and more of an indicator of true writing ability, it's not. A 45-minute essay is hardly a good way to measure one's competence and the truth is, those who go in prepared with a good idea of what they're going to write do better than those who don't.

The ACT is simply not the place for you to get fancy. There will be plenty of opportunities later on, whether you want them or not, to express yourself more creatively. The ACT is not one of them. Your purpose is to ace it and get into college, not start the next great American novel.

Having said all that, let's take a look at the characteristics of a perfect essay.

1. Length

Most students don't realize just how much essay length affects the score. You might think that a short essay can compensate for its length by being well-written, but while quality does count, you're much better off sacrificing some of that quality for a longer essay. In a 2005 *New York Times* article, writer Michael Winerip reports how Dr. Les Perelman, one of the directors of writing at MIT, posted student essays on a far wall and graded them solely on length. After he finished, he was stunned by the results—his predictions had been right over 90 percent of the time. The shorter essays received the lowest scores and the longer essays received the highest. Even though his study was done with SAT essays, the results apply just as much to the ACT. Write longer essays. More often that not, an essay's score can be determined by its length. It's no coincidence that my first essay, which scored a 36, was longer than my second essay, which scored a 32.

With that in mind, you want to fill up as much space as you can, at least 2.5 pages (which actually isn't a lot given the line spacing). Filling up 2.5 pages means you have to **write fast from the start**. Minimal brainstorming. No wasting time. Just go. **You want to spend every minute writing.**

Now this doesn't mean you should start lengthening the spacing between words. The graders are wary of essays that inflate their spacing and from my students' experiences, it definitely doesn't work. Write how you would normally but do so at a much faster pace. My essay in Appendix A shows the degree of illegibility you can get away with.

2. Thesis

As you probably have learned countless times from your English classes, a thesis is a statement that captures the main idea or essence of your argument. It's usually placed at the end of the introductory paragraph.

Always have a thesis statement because it's something graders can easily spot and reward you for. A grader should be able to grasp your stance on the issue just by reading your thesis. I'll be teaching you how to write effective and easy thesis statements in the next chapter.

3. Organization and Structure

Always make sure you use paragraphs and that each paragraph serves a purpose that is distinct from the others. In other words, each of your paragraphs should contain a different idea but one that still relates to the overall argument.

Essays that are just one humongous paragraph don't get high scores, so make sure you indent!

4. Vocabulary

People judge essays by the level of their vocabulary. If you've ever thought of a book or article more highly because there were words you didn't understand, then you probably know just how much vocabulary can impress people, and the ACT essay graders are no exception. After all, good essays are good in part because they have sophisticated yet well-chosen words. Later on, we will be showing you not only what words to use but also some automatic ways of injecting them into your essay.

On the flip side, avoid using vague words like "stuff", "things", "lots of", "many cases", "many reasons", especially when you don't clarify them later with specifics.

5. Sentence Variety

Good writers use a mix of simple and complex sentences. Essays consisting solely of simple sentences won't get you a high score. Imagine reading a paragraph like this:

> People are most productive under pressure. They have to think faster. They work harder to meet deadlines. Most people are lazy. They need motivation. Pressure is the best motivator.

Choppy and repetitive—not what you want. Let's take a look at a revised version:

> People are most productive under pressure because they have to think faster and work harder to meet deadlines. Without motivation, most people are lazy. For those reasons, pressure is the best motivator.

Still not perfect, but a whole lot better. Notice that the main ideas didn't change, only the way in which they were connected.

By definition, the secret to creating complex sentences is **the comma**. By finding appropriate ways to insert commas, you force yourself to add detail to your sentences. Let's use an example sentence to see how this is done:

> The tiger ate my aunt earlier today.

Now let's add in some phrases:

> After starving for several hours, the tiger, which had previously been so tame, ate my aunt earlier today.

Notice that by adding in those phrases, which required commas, **we not only made the sentence complex but also made it more detailed, which is part of what good writing is all about.**

Here is a toolbox of things you can do for sentence variety:

Tool	Example
Use *because*	The tiger ate my aunt earlier today because it was hungry.
Use *who, which,* or *that*	The tiger, which had been very hungry, ate my aunt earlier today.
Use a conjunction (FANBOYS)	The tiger was hungry and ate my aunt earlier today.
Put *although/even though* in front	Although it is usually well-behaved, the tiger ate my aunt earlier today.
Use a modifier	Always on the lookout for food, the tiger ate my aunt earlier today.

As you practice, make it a point to put complex sentences among simple ones.

6. Transitions

One other weapon in your sentence variety toolbox is transitions, the words that show how your ideas are connected. These are so important to getting a high score that they deserve their own section. If you look at the official essay rubric on the ACT's website, graders are specifically required to look for them. Not only do they serve as the "glue" between your ideas, but they also give your sentencess rhythm and structure.

Common Transition Words		
Example	**Transition...**	**Similar Transitions**
I love eating vanilla ice cream. **However**, *too much of it makes me sick.*	presents an opposing point or balances a previous statement	*fortunately, on the other hand, conversely, whereas, while, in contrast*
Math trains you to approach problems more analytically. **Furthermore**, *it helps you calculate the exact amount of tip to be left for the waiter.*	adds new and supporting information	*in addition, also, moreover, and, too, as well, additionally, not to mention*
Pandas are rapidly becoming extinct. **In fact**, *some experts predict that pandas will die out in 50 years.*	gives emphasis to a point by adding a specific detail/case	*as a matter of fact, indeed, to illustrate, for instance, for example*
The state is facing a flu epidemic. **Consequently**, *all hospital rooms are filled at the moment.*	shows cause & effect	*as a result, because, hence, therefore, thus, as a consequence, accordingly*
Granted, *the ACT is a long and tedious exam, but it's necessary for college admissions.*	concedes a point to make way for your own point	*nevertheless, although, even though, despite, even if*
Place the bread on an ungreased baking sheet. **Finally**, *bake in a preheated oven for 10 minutes.*	shows order or sequence	*subsequently, previously, afterwards, next, then, eventually, before*
Social security numbers uniquely identify citizens. **In the same way**, *IP addresses identify computers.*	shows similarity	*similarly, likewise, by the same token*
In conclusion, *the world would be a happier place without nuclear weapons.*	gives a summary	*in all, to summarize, in sum, to sum up, in short, as mentioned, thus*

You'll want to include several transition words in your essay to show the grader that you understand their importance and how they're used. The essay template in the next chapter will give you easy ways to add both transitions and sentence variety to your essay.

4

The Essay Template for any Prompt

Now that you've learned what constitutes a perfect essay, this chapter will introduce a repeatable framework that will make essay writing easy. After all, an essay is more than just examples; there needs to be an underlying structure that organizes them. This is THE template that my students and I have used to get perfect scores. It may seem complicated and hard to memorize at first, but if you actually practice it a few times, you'll see how easy it is to produce amazing essays.

Note that the template requires two examples, one for each of the first two body paragraphs. We'll talk more about example generation in later chapters, but for now, just keep in mind that Examples 1 and 2 will ideally come from a bank of prepared examples.

Also note how many transitions and college-level words are automatically integrated into this template. Familiarize yourself with them. Look up any words you don't know. My comments are italicized.

Introduction

The notion that   Noun 1   reflects/leads to/breeds/requires/stifles   Noun 2   has its roots in   Subject , but its underpinnings are often overlooked. (*The purpose of this opening sentence is to cast doubt on the opposing stance. The gray boxes represent blanks to be filled in by you.*)

While   Statement supporting opposing stance ,   Statement supporting your stance .

In fact,   Follow-up statement .

Even with all the societal friction   Noun 1   may engender,   Thesis stating your stance .

Body Paragraph 1

Take, for example, Example 1 .

> Storyline/Details of Example 1 (*at least 6 sentences*)
> Ensure Example 1 relates to Thesis (*2-3 sentences if necessary*)

While some may argue that Counter argument , actually Your rebuttal . (*This sentence forces you to consider another perspective and relate everything back to your thesis.*)

Body Paragraph 2

In the same way Example 1 general statement , Example 2 general statement . (*This is a transition from the first paragraph to the second. Remember that you are graded on whether you have paragraph transitions.*)

> Storyline/Details of Example 2 (*at least 6 sentences*)
> Ensure Example 2 relates to Thesis (*2-3 sentences if necessary*)

Without Noun , Bad consequence . (*This sentence is amazing. Not only does it force you to come back to the thesis, but it also strengthens your argument by indicating what would happen in an opposing scenario.*)

Body Paragraph 3

Still, detractors/proponents of Noun assert that General statement . (*Another paragraph transition. Notice how many college-level words are built in for you!*)

> Reasons (*2-3 sentences. You're arguing for another perspective here. To get a perfect score, you must weave in the other perspectives. The third body paragraph is the best place to do so.*)

However, what these critics/supporters fail to consider is Your rebuttal argument . (*Now you turn the tables on the previous perspectives and reinforce to the reader why your perspective is the right one.*)

> Your reasons (*at least 3 sentences*)

Conclusion

As exemplified by | Example 1 | and | Example 2 |, | Thesis Restatement |.

Ultimately, | Lesson the reader should learn from your essay |.

If we all adopted that view/lesson/attitude, society would be more conducive to innovation/good citizenship/progress. (*The conclusion is essentially written for you. No matter what prompt you get, this conclusion will work.*)

At this point, you're probably very confused and overwhelmed. Don't worry! Using my very own essay, I'll illustrate how exactly this template is used, but first, the December 2015 prompt (rephrased to avoid copyright issues):

Time Away from Tech

In today's society, we are tied to our digital devices in many ways. We use our phones to text and take pictures, our computers to type up reports and spreadsheets, and our televisions to watch shows and play games. Technology is such an ingrained part of our everyday life that it's hard to disconnect from the digital world. In fact, we've become so dependent on electronic devices that many people are now alarmed. They warn of the damage this dependence can inflict on our health, relationships, and sense of self. To curb our constant need to be connected, they recommend that we intentionally set aside time to be spent away from technology. Because of the increasing presence of technology in our lives, it is important that we examine whether some time away from tech would be beneficial.

Read and carefully consider these perspectives. Each suggests a particular way of thinking about whether we should spend time away from technology.

Perspective One	Perspective Two	Perspective Three
Connection to technology is the very definition of modern society. It's pointless to act as if we do not depend on and take pleasure from the digital world.	We should spend time away from technology to reconnect with ourselves. Digital devices disconnect us from and make it hard to appreciate the real world.	Many people can't disconnect even if they tried. Their lives and relationships are too reliant on their devices, or they're just too addicted to give them up.

Essay Task

Write a unified, coherent essay in which you evaluate multiple perspectives on the conflict between safety and privacy. In your essay, be sure to:
- analyze and evaluate the perspectives given
- state and develop your own perspective on the issue
- explain the relationship between your perspective and those given

Your perspective may be in full agreement with any of the others, in partial agreement, or wholly different. Whatever the case, support your ideas with logical reasoning and detailed, persuasive examples.

Now I'm going to be honest—I'm not a naturally talented writer. I was a solid B student in most of my high school English classes. But by using the template in this chapter, I was able get a perfect score with a minute to spare. The following is the typed-up version, word-for-word (see Appendix A for a copy of the original hand-written version). Try to spot each component of the template in this essay.

My Perfect 36 Essay from the December 2015 ACT Exam

The notion that technology will doom mankind has its roots in ominous sci-fi movies and novels but its underpinnings are often overlooked. While it is true that modern society is becoming increasingly dependent on devices such as cell phones, this dependency should not be frowned upon. In fact, many of technology's capabilities allow us to experience the world in ways we never could've imagined. Even with all the societal friction technological devices may engender, the benefits outweigh the costs and we should embrace our digital world, not fight it.

Take, for example, the many applications available on cell phones today. These "apps," such as facebook, uber, and airbnb connect us in ways that were previously impossible. Facebook allows us to chat with friends and family halfway across the world. Uber connects drivers looking for part time income with daily commuters at the click of a button. Airbnb allows homeowners who have an empty room to profit from a tourist or visitor who prefers a more local experience than that of a hotel, which is often more expensive. In fact, airbnb found places to stay for more than 50,000 visitors in Brazil during the 2014 World Cup. Furthermore, in times of emergency, it is these very apps that get criticized for disconnecting us from reality that provide updates and the locations of safe havens. While some may argue that we spend more time with these devices than friends and even family, much to our detriment, actually they connect us to friends and family even more. We should welcome this enhanced connection instead of avoiding it.

In the same way that cell phones open up new ways for society to connect, companies are ushering in new possibilities through technology and our devices. Amazon, the online retail site, now makes it easy to order everything from books to mattresses from the comfort of one's home. No longer are we confined to the limited section at the local bookstore. This widespread availability of books, music, and products fosters the spread of ideas and promotes the work of artists and writers who may have been invisible otherwise. Writers like Amanda Hocking and others have self-published their work to great success. In addition to Amazon, search engines like Google open up a world of information not limited by the scope of an encyclopedia. By democratizing information and enabling users to share it, these sites serve as portals of connection, not isolation. Without technology and the devices we use, we would be stripped of the enrichment that websites like Amazon and Google could provide.

Still, technology's detractors assert that our dependency stifles our relationships with those in our presence. After all, who doesn't have a friend who's seemingly addicted to texting and online shopping? What these critics fail to consider is that there is more communication now than ever before and to remove oneself from the digital world is to experience the very solitary condition they detest. Indeed, much of society has already embraced the benefits of technology and there is very little that can turn us back. Many families have already disconnected their land lines in favor of cell phones. Many malls and retail stores have closed, failing to compete with their online rivals, for better or worse. Many books are now being read on "e-readers" such as the Kindle or Nook. Our cars today come equipped with GPS, and many would feel lost without them. The world has already embraced these devices and our dependency should not be resisted.

As exemplified by many cell phone apps such as airbnb and sites like Amazon and Google, the benefits of digital devices outweigh the costs, and in fact, open up more avenues for human connection. Ultimately, we should not take up arms against technology but welcome it. If we all adopted that view, our society would be more conducive to innovation and progress.

Step-by-step

Notice how closely my essay follows the template prescribed in this chapter. All the examples I used were ones that I had planned out and memorized beforehand. There is absolutely no way I would've been able to crank out that essay in 40 minutes if I didn't have something scripted in advance. Here's my step by step process when I first open the writing booklet:

1. Read the informational paragraph at the beginning of the prompt. It only takes 30 seconds and it gives you context for what you'll be writing. It might also help you think of the examples you'll use in your essay.

2. Read the three perspectives.

3. Get to the core issue (we'll talk about this later).

4. Choose one of the three perspectives to be your own stance, typically the one that you have the most examples to support. Keep in mind you only need 2 good examples. You can also choose a perspective that's different from the three, but only do so if the examples you have in mind are better suited for it. It's easier to work with three perspectives than four.

5. Come up with the two examples you'll use to support your chosen perspective. Hopefully, you can draw from your bank of prepared examples. Later chapters will give you some versatile examples you can use as well as some ways of generating examples when you're stuck.

6. Don't read the essay task—it's always the same. You should know from practice what the assignment is.

7. At this point, it's time to start your essay. You should be putting pencil to paper within 5 minutes of the starting time.

8. It's pretty smooth sailing once the essay starts coming together in your mind. Just follow the template for the body paragraphs and the conclusion.

9. Always always have a conclusion. The graders will punish you if you don't have one. I'd rather cut one of my body paragraphs short than run out of time before the conclusion. It's completely scripted out for you in the template so just bang it out when you have 3-4 minutes left. Like the introduction, the conclusion should be muscle memory.

The beauty of having a template is that it takes the thinking away from all the essay components that relate to organization, vocabulary, and transitions, allowing you to focus your time and attention on the examples and making them as relevant to your thesis as possible. Furthermore, it ensures that your essay has sentence variety and that you consider more than one perspective.

This template essentially makes a low score nearly impossible because even if your examples aren't very strong, you'll still score high on the *Organization* and *Language Use and Conventions* categories that make up your score.

Some Frequently Asked Questions

1. *I've been taught all my life to write an awesome hook that draws the reader in. Doesn't the hook in the template seem a bit generic?*

   First of all, the introductory sentence is amazing because it uses college-level vocabulary in an intelligent way to lead into the topic. No other type of hook will impress the graders more. Remember that they're hired to rush through hundreds of essays full of poor writing and made-up examples from students everywhere. There is NO hook in the ENTIRE world that would excite them. I'm a teacher myself and I've read hundreds of essays from students taking mock tests for the first time. The best they've been able to get from me is a chuckle (usually from terrible hooks). Maybe I'm just a mean, humorless teacher, but still...

   Don't go out of your way and waste 5 minutes coming up with an awesome hook. Even if you manage to come up with an ingenious attention-grabber, it's just one sentence in your entire essay. The hook alone will not get you a perfect score. Writing a long intelligent essay will.

2. *Will the graders know I'm using a template?*

   Graders look at so many essays that it's extremely unlikely they'll be able to tell whether you're using a template. None of my students have ever been penalized for using the template in this book (or any other template). Even if the graders somehow knew you were using this specific template from this specific book, they would still have to base their grades on the essay content and NOT on whether they think you used a template. If you're still concerned, then I recommend you develop your own introductory sentence. The first sentence is more likely to tip a grader off than anything else from the template. This leads me to the next question...

3. *Can I tweak the template to fit my own style/needs?*

   Absolutely. Everything in the template is a guideline. The main point is to go in prepared with something you can rattle off immediately. Some of my students, given any prompt you throw at them, can map out an entire essay in seconds.

4. *Do I need to practice?*

   Um yes! Keep writing essays until you can consistently churn out high quality responses. Do not think that it'll come easy just because you read this chapter. So many students, including my younger self, think that they can pull off a great essay just by reading some formula or template. Then when test day inevitably rolls around, they freeze up and totally botch it. Having the template in your mind is not the same as being able to write it. You need to make it muscle memory. Go and practice.

6 Versatile Essay Examples

For the template to work, you need to have well-thought-out examples to support your points. The problem most students have is that they can't come up with examples on the spot. And even when they're able to, they find it hard to give specific details because they don't know the examples well enough. The result is writer's block, shallow writing, and ultimately low scores.

That's why you should always go into the test with a bank of prepared examples. It allows you to minimize the time you spend thinking about what to write.

This chapter contains 6 versatile examples you can use to start off your bank of prepared examples. The best essay examples are ones that have a good side and a dark side, making them easy to tweak to support whatever argument you're making. While the following examples should serve you well in many of the prompts you'll encounter, it will pay off to come up with your own. You might also find it helpful to memorize your 4-5 prepared examples using an acronym. So if you wanted to have *apps, obesity, loneliness,* and *global warming* as your go-to examples, you might use the acronym AOLG: All Ostriches Like Games.

Disclaimer: The following examples are the ones I personally count on and they should work for many of the prompts you might see. However, they will not be usable for every single one. I can't predict all the weird prompts the ACT might throw at you. You should be willing to put in the work to come up with a few of your own examples and stay flexible should you encounter a tough topic. A later chapter will cover what to do when your prepared examples don't fit the prompt.

1. Apps/Websites

Uber

- A ride-sharing/taxi service that allows passengers to hail a driver from an app
- Offers rides at typically lower prices than those of traditional taxis and even lower prices for those who share rides with other passengers who are picked up along the way
- Banned from several places including Germany, India, and Japan for avoiding local taxi regulations
- Faces a multitude of lawsuits from taxi companies that now face stiff competition from independent Uber drivers
- Doesn't provide health insurance or retirement benefits to its drivers, treating them as contractors rather than employees

AirBnB

- An app that connects homeowners to visitors who are looking to rent a spare room or an apartment for a short stay
- Allows travelers to get an experience that is more local and cheaper than staying at a hotel
- 50,000 visitors to Brazil were housed through AirBnB during the 2016 World Cup
- Like Uber, AirBnB faces many lawsuits over property regulations. For example, tenants in New York City are operating their rentals as illegal hotels, which violate not only the lease agreements but also the fire alarm and exit requirements
- Faces safety and liability concerns about letting strangers into homes. All hosts and guests are supposedly vetted through AirBnB's profile and review system.

Amazon

- A reliable and trustworthy retail site that prides itself on unlimited selection and discounted prices
- Takes advantage of physical retail stores: consumers check out the product in person but then buy on Amazon at a lower price
- Has signed exclusive deals for certain products so that consumers have no other purchasing options
- Bullies suppliers. For example, Hachette, a large publisher, demanded control over the price of its ebooks on Amazon. Amazon complied but only after removing discounts on Hachette's books and increasing their shipping time.
- Will sometimes sell products at a loss to gain market share

Google

- The world's most used search engine
- Democratizes and promotes the spread of information by making it openly accessible in an organized way
- Tracks and uses your search history to develop your user profile, which it sells to third parties who then target you for ads. For example, the travel site Orbitz raised prices for hotels on Google users who were on an Apple computer.
- Criticized for being an "arbiter of truth." For example, Google Maps refers to Taiwan as a "Province of China" when there is actually ongoing political controversy over who controls the region. Many people believe Taiwan is an independent nation and criticize Google for seemingly taking sides.

2. Obesity Epidemic

The Centers for Disease Control reports that one-third of American adults are obese and two-thirds are overweight. Childhood obesity rates have tripled since the 1980s, raising concerns that overall obesity rates will continue to rise as these children reach adulthood—unless something is done to reverse the trend. Widespread obesity is costly, leading to decreased quality of life and preventable deaths from such associated conditions as heart disease and type-2 diabetes. The CDC estimated in 2008 that the annual medical cost of obesity in the United States was $150 billion, with obese individuals averaging over $1400 more per year than persons of normal weight. How did this happen? And what can be done to stem the tide?

The simplest explanation for the increase in obesity is the imbalance between the intake of calories and the burning of calories. If a person consumes more calories than his or her body actually uses, then weight gain will result. A combination of factors has led to this imbalance. One is the increasingly sedentary lifestyle of most Americans in comparison with previous generations. While one hundred years ago people walked to work, walked to school, and performed tasks throughout the day that required physical exertion, cars are now the primary form of transportation, fewer jobs require physical labor, and fewer people perform physically demanding chores. Plus, children tend to stay indoors during free time, playing video games and watching television, unlike their predecessors who played mostly outside.

In addition to increased exercise, fundamental changes in diet are necessary to reduce obesity. The second half of the twentieth century saw a revolution in eating habits, as people increasingly ate processed foods high in carbohydrates—particularly refined sugars like high-fructose corn syrup that supply an overabundance of calories. These leftover calories from sugar are converted to fat, leading to weight gain. In the 1970s, it was recommended that people observe a low-fat diet; ironically, this led to an explosion in weight gain as people replaced fats in their diets with carbohydrates. It takes fewer calories from fatty foods to make a person feel full than calories from sugary foods. Therefore, a transition away from high-carb, processed foods like fast food, soft drinks, and most snack foods toward a diet based on plants and high-fat, high-protein foods will likely reduce the obesity trend, especially if combined with an increase in physical activity. As consumption and burning of calories balance out, the health costs and suffering will decrease.

3. Loneliness in America

In 2006, The American Sociological Association reported that rates of loneliness in America had tripled over the previous twenty years. Despite increasing connectedness through social media networks like Facebook, Twitter, and Instagram, loneliness has continued to increase to the point that some are predicting it could become a national health crisis. A study at Brigham Young University found that feelings of loneliness increased the risk of death by 26%, leading numerous online publications, including CNN, The Huffington Post, and The Guardian to raise the alarm about a possible rising tide of isolation and suicide, particularly among young Americans.

The reasons for the increase in loneliness are complex. The past several decades have seen unprecedented shifts in lifestyle. Just two generations ago, few people owned televisions, and watching television was a family activity. Now, it's common for multiple people in a family to have their own personal television or electronic device on which to watch whatever entertainment they prefer. Just a few decades ago, video games did not exist, but now the Entertainment Software Association reports that 80% of American homes contain devices for playing video games and that around half of Americans play video games on a weekly basis, with many of them playing for several hours a week. With parents increasingly concerned about the safety of their children, fewer children play outside with friends on a regular basis, ensuring that they spend more time inside enjoying electronic entertainment by themselves.

Entertainment is just one part of the shift. In past times, shopping involved visiting a local market, grocer, or store and encountering the same vendors and fellow shoppers on a regular basis. Now, with big box stores and online stores replacing small retailers and grocers, the shopping experience has become anonymous. It also used to be common for people to remain at the same workplace for many years, but now it is more common to switch jobs. Plus, for many Americans, church was once a central source of community, but now fewer Americans attend church regularly.

Reversing the trend in loneliness will cost both time and money. It costs more to buy food from farmers' markets and goods from local businesses. Involvement in a church or other social organization is time-consuming and challenging relationally. It takes time, energy, and money to invite people over for dinner, to involve children in social activities outside of school, and to create regular family times. However, these costs in time, energy, and money are worth paying if we are to foster community and defeat loneliness.

4. Global Warming

The Earth is getting warmer, but are humans to blame? Most of modern life is powered by fossil fuels like coal and oil, which, when burned, emit carbon dioxide that traps heat as it is released into the atmosphere. Coal is the primary source of electricity around the world, and oil is used to make plastic and the fuels that power vehicles and machinery worldwide.

The Fourth Assessment Report of the Intergovernmental Panel on Climate Change, published in 2007, claims that there is at least a 90% certainty that global warming has derived mostly from increases in man-made emissions of carbon dioxide gas. Carbon molecules released by the burning of fossil fuels weigh less than other carbon molecules in the atmosphere, and measurements of carbon levels in the atmosphere have shown an increase in these lighter carbon molecules, which correlates with the overall increase in carbon dioxide emissions and in the global temperature. As a result of this research, the vast majority of scientists have concluded that humans are responsible for most of the global warming that has occurred over the past century.

Climate change could produce such harmful effects worldwide that many politicians and activists have called for a severe reduction in carbon emissions throughout the world. Sea levels are rising as polar ice caps melt, and water levels could eventually rise high enough to cause catastrophic flooding in coastal regions. Moreover, equatorial regions could turn into semi-deserts where growing crops becomes almost impossible. These two consequences would be most severe for third-world countries and their populations. As a result, wealthier nations must consider the effects of their fossil-fuel driven economies and make the well-being of poorer countries a priority as they address climate change.

Many politicians are unwilling to acknowledge human causes behind climate change. This is because the proposed solutions involve severe cuts in carbon emissions that would require us to depend on unreliable forms of energy, such as solar and wind power. In the end, however, the preservation of the Earth's environment must take the highest priority. It's possible that a warmer planet that reaps the benefits of fossil fuels will be preferable to the alternative. But if that is the case, opponents of capping carbon emissions must be able to address how coastal and equatorial regions will thrive in the midst of global warming.

5. STEM Education and the Gender Gap

In recent years, growing concerns about shortages in American STEM workers has led to initiatives to reverse this trend. STEM stands for science, technology, engineering, and mathematics, and President Obama has pledged hundreds of millions of dollars to boost STEM education in the United States. With American students' test scores in math and science lagging behind their peers' internationally, the President has identified a national crisis in education that could stifle economic growth for years to come.

There are reasons, however, to temper the alarmist rhetoric of the President and the press. The New York Academy of Sciences published a report in January 2015 that revealed what they term "the global STEM paradox." STEM graduates, the report found, outnumber the available STEM jobs, yet there remains a shortage of workers for these jobs. While a lack of skilled technicians has contributed greatly to the shortage, the report identifies a more fundamental problem: the lack of "soft skills" among STEM graduates. Many students' weaknesses in critical thinking, communication, and interpersonal skills prevent them from successfully transitioning out of the classroom and into the workforce.

As the perception grows that the US needs more STEM students, calls continually arise to divert funding away from humanities programs. The humanities, they say, cannot justify their existence, since they do not produce job-ready graduates or drive the economy. Yet, given the shortage of students with sufficient soft skills to fill the STEM jobs that drive innovation, a humanities-integrated education may be exactly what future scientists need.

Furthermore, the perceived shortage of STEM workers may be related to the gender gap—although women fill close to half of all jobs in the U.S. economy, they hold less than 25 percent of STEM jobs. While this gap may be attributable more to a cultural issue—girls are raised to be more interested in the humanities than in STEM—many women have claimed that working in "a boy's club" is uncomfortable. Other contributing factors include a lack of female role models, gender stereotyping, and less family-friendly flexibility in STEM fields. To close the gap, many tech companies are now trying to promote more diversity in the workplace and push for equal opportunities for women. Colleges are encouraging more women to go into STEM fields by hiring more female faculty and providing more funding to female researchers.

6. Student Loan Debt Crisis

Student loan debt has been steadily growing over the last several decades and is now one of the largest economic problems within the nation. In the mid 1990s, the average student loan was about $10,000. Today, that number is about $35,000. The reason for this increase is the quadrupling of tuition in the last thirty-five years, which in turn was driven by the surge in college attendance—the number of students has doubled since 1995. Although public subsidies have risen, they still cannot keep up with the number of people attending college. Therefore, funding per student has decreased while tuition has increased. Instead of federal and state governments providing the necessary monetary support as they did in the past, families are now the ones who must bear the financial burden.

Universities have also expanded their administrations significantly, further increasing the cost of college. As they compete fiercely for students in the age of college rankings, they've started to operate almost as for-profit companies. Indeed, a great education has taken a back seat to luxury housing, gyms, and recreation centers, all of which are marketed heavily to students. Meanwhile, professors are being replaced by teaching assistants and budgets for new classroom equipment are shrinking. Critics have condemned the predatory practices now being used by university administrators to enroll students. Those who cannot afford another semester are being encouraged to take out hundreds of thousands of dollars in loans to finish their degrees, and high school students are getting flyers in the mail from colleges they have no chance of getting in to, all so the universities can brag about their large pools of applicants and low acceptance rates.

The universities are not fully to blame for the debt crisis, however. Part of the responsibility falls on the students themselves. Many take out huge loans with the unrealistic belief that they can major in anything and be able to pay them off later. In addition, they often neglect to learn the financial knowledge needed to make informed decisions about college spending. A study involving five hundred students found that less than 8% of the participants knew what their interest rates were and 96% did not know loans could be refinanced after graduation. Students today are very unaware of their borrowing and what it takes to pay it off after graduation.

The rise in student debt has had a major impact on the economy. Nationwide, total student debt surpassed the $1 trillion mark in 2012 and now stands at $1.2 trillion. This level of debt is limiting the ability of graduates to cover life's expenses—cars, houses, health, investments—and preventing them from starting new businesses or switching careers. Efforts are being made to help reverse the current trend, but full recovery will depend on educating students on how to be financially independent while they're still in school.

6

Getting to the Core Issue

Nearly all ACT essay prompts can be reduced to one of the following two questions:

- Should we have _____ ?
- What does _____ say about _____ ?

I call the central question of each essay its **core issue**.

Why did we give this topic its own chapter? Because it's that important.

Too many students make the mistake of choosing examples that don't actually support their main argument. The problem is that they don't know what they're arguing for in the first place. Breaking down the prompt into its core issue will help you stay on track and ensure that your examples are actually relevant to your argument. Make it a habit to identify the core issue for every ACT essay you write.

Here are some examples of core issues:

- Should we have vocational training in schools?
- Should we have tech-free time?
- Should we have sports in schools?
- Should we have limits to freedom for the sake of health?
- What does the trend towards casual dress say about our values?
- What does free music say about how much we value it today?
- What does declining event attendance say about our cultural values?

What's the difference between the core issue and your chosen perspective? The core issue is a question. Your perspective/stance is your answer to that question. Defining what the core issue is will help you develop your perspective in a way that sticks to the prompt.

What to Do When All Your Examples Fail

Imagine this scenario. You've got at least a few prepared examples down cold and you walk into the test confident that you'll be able to tweak them to fit the prompt. You get to the writing section, open the test booklet, read the perspectives, identify the core issue, and then a knot forms in your stomach—you just know none of your examples apply to the prompt. You take a deep breath for the long road ahead.

There's a good chance you'll be in this situation at some point, either in practice or during the real test.

When it happens in practice, you really need to ask yourself whether you actually know your examples inside and out. Many students don't put in the time required to understand their go-to examples; they only have a superficial understanding. Within any example, there are many nuances that you can discuss. These nuances are what allow you to tweak the example in clever ways to fit the prompt. If you're not aware of them, the number of prompts your examples can be adapted to will be limited.

For instance, let's say Amazon is one of my go-to examples. If the only thing I know about Amazon is that it's an online retail site that has a huge variety of products, then I'm in trouble. But if I also know that they bully their suppliers, engage in monopolistic pricing behavior, poach employees from other tech companies, and take advantage of retail stores, then suddenly Amazon becomes an example I can apply to a lot more topics.

The second thing you need to consider when you freeze up is how much you've actually practiced. To learn how to tweak your examples and discuss them in an intelligent way, you must go through the experience of having used them in timed practice essays. Applying your examples is a skill. It's not enough to just have them in your head. Once you've actually used your examples in a written essay, using them again is much easier because many of the sentences become muscle memory and you're able to carry over the same details. I know it's painful to sit down for 40 minutes at a time and write essays that aren't required for school, but these rehearsals will prevent freeze-ups and get you through your body paragraphs quickly and smoothly on test day.

To summarize, the majority of essay panic attacks stem from a superficial understanding of the prepared examples and a lack of practice. Don't be lazy.

Ok, so you have your examples down and you've done your practice. Even now, you might still get stumped by a prompt on the real test. After all, there's nothing that prevents oddball topics like reality TV or musical instruments from showing up.

If you do get stumped on the real test, don't panic. The first thing you should do is double-check whether your go-to examples apply. You might think they don't, but in many cases, they do. Here are two ways they might apply:

1. The topic solves a problem that happens to be one of your examples.

Let's say you come across a prompt in which the central issue is whether sports should be an essential part of schooling (this was the February 2016 prompt). If you were writing this essay, you might think none of the examples from the last chapter apply. After all, none of them discuss an actual sport or athlete. However, with a little thinking, two of them turn out to be perfect examples for this prompt: obesity and loneliness.

Why?

Because sports is a solution to both the obesity problem and the loneliness problem. Sports encourages students to be physically active while strengthening the bonds among teammates and friends. In writing this essay, you would discuss obesity in the first body paragraph and loneliness in the second.

2. Your examples are better suited to an opposing side or another perspective.

Sometimes getting your examples to fit is just a matter of choosing a different perspective. Some perspectives simply aren't geared for the example-based approach, requiring a more logical approach instead. You'll want to avoid choosing those perspectives.

So let's say you're confronted with the same prompt about sports, but you didn't have obesity and loneliness in your bank of go-to examples. How would you then use the remaining examples from the last chapter to argue that sports should be promoted in schools. Well, that's tough. Our remaining examples are apps, global warming, STEM education, and Enron. None of them can realistically be used to support our argument.

But consider what happens if we argue that sports should not be promoted in schools. Indeed, one of the perspectives from the February 2016 prompt was that sports distracts students by shifting their focus away from academics. If we argued for this opposing perspective, STEM education as an example would suddenly be an option. We could argue that the shortage of workers in math, science, and technology, subjects that require a lot of time and dedication, reflects the extent to which our sports culture is getting in the way of young boys and girls becoming scientists and engineers. Therefore, sports should not be promoted in school.

The only caveat here is that we shouldn't turn our entire essay into an argument supporting STEM education. There is a fine line between arguing against sports and arguing for STEM education. For example, don't start talking about how we need STEM education so that people understand our increasingly technological world. That's straying too far from sports and would completely switch the topic of the essay. This is a common mistake that we'll discuss in more detail in the next chapter.

Other Options

If your mind is still blank at this point, you still have many options:

1. Brainstorm examples outside your prepared ones

Once I'm thrown outside my bank of prepared examples, my process is to quickly think of ideas and then write about them using the five W's: who, what, when, where, and why.

- **Who** is the example. It does not have to be a person. It can be a thing or an event.

- **What** relevant background information can I provide about the example?

- **When** does not have to refer to any specific dates. It can be opportunity to talk about past vs. present or how your example has evolved or will continue to evolve over time.

- **Where** does everything take place?

- **Why** is this example important? **How** does it support my chosen perspective?

The key here is to come up with examples that you can still discuss in detail. So let's say that I wanted to use Psy, the Korean rapper, to support the perspective that we value music more today because it's cheaper and more accessible (an official prompt, by the way). Here's an example of how I would use the 5 W's to figure out what to include in my body paragraph:

- **Who:** Psy, the Korean rapper

- **What:** Psy created the k-pop hit song *Gangnam Style*, which features amusing dance moves that became a global phenomenon. His music video was the first YouTube video to reach one billion views.

- **When:** The song was written in 2012. Its popularity was made possible by social media and free online distribution. Psy's global reach would not have been possible before the Internet.

- **Where:** Many people started exploring Korean culture and its music because of *Gangnam Style*'s popularity.

- **Why & How:** The immense popularity of *Gangnam Style* is evidence of the increasing value of music. Music now has a larger impact on our lives because of its accessibility through technology. In using free online channels such as YouTube, we come to appreciate new genres and even new cultures.

If I don't think I have enough background information on a topic to be able to answer the 5 W's, I won't use it as an example.

2. Use several, small-scale examples

The examples I lay out in this book are all big issues (global warming, obesity, etc.), but that doesn't mean your examples have to be. If you're struggling to find one big example to fill out a body paragraph, try using several small-scale examples instead.

Now what do I mean by small-scale examples?

Well, if we're arguing that people no longer respect each other, we might bring up the uncultured comments on YouTube, texting in front of others, and phone conversations in front of customers. If we're arguing that we need to embrace technology instead of trying to free ourselves from it, we could bring up all the devices we depend on—GPS in cars, smartphones that double as music players, computers at work and school, automated check-out registers, online banking. None of these examples are significant enough on their own to fill up an entire paragraph (assuming you don't anything beyond the basics) but together they make a strong case.

Here's what a paragraph using this approach might look like:

> Take, for example, all the devices that are ubiquitous in our lives. Smartphones allow us to contact loved ones in times of emergency. On those very same devices we can use apps to hail taxis and find the right directions. The Internet allows us to pay our bills without having to visit the bank or post office, and we can watch sporting events on television instead of paying for expensive tickets. All of these devices serve an important role in navigating modern life. We should embrace them for their benefits instead of avoiding them out of a sense of dependence. After all, it's now more of a burden to live without technology than to live with it. Not only do our friends use these devices to communicate but most jobs today require technical computer skills. Although some may say that we have an addiction to electronic devices that is unhealthy, these devices are part of our lives because they've improved our the standard of living just as cars and trains have since they were first introduced.

Notice that there isn't one over-arching example but a string of minor ones that all serve as evidence.

3. Base your examples off of the prompt's setup paragraph

When you're trying to come up with examples big or small, the prompt's setup paragraph can provide much-needed inspiration. Every ACT essay prompt starts off with a paragraph that sets up the three perspectives. This paragraph almost always refers to topics and examples that relate to the issue. While you shouldn't copy directly from this paragraph, you are certainly allowed to bring up those same topics and examples in your essay.

Let's use the December 2015 prompt as an example. The setup paragraph from that prompt is shown below:

In today's society, we are tied to our digital devices in many ways. We use our phones to text and take pictures, our computers to type up reports and spreadsheets, and our televisions to watch shows and play games. Technology is such an ingrained part of our everyday life that it's hard to disconnect from the digital world. In fact, we've become so dependent on electronic devices that many people are now alarmed. They warn of the damage this dependence can inflict on our health, relationships, and sense of self. To curb our constant need to be connected, they recommend that we intentionally set aside time to be spent away from technology. Because of the increasing presence of technology in our lives, it is important that we examine whether some time away from tech would be beneficial.

I've underlined the portion that brings up examples and topics that you can use. Based on this sentence, you might bring up television show binge-watching as an example to elaborate on, or you might talk about how digital tools such as spreadsheets force businesses to be dependent on software. Obviously, a little creativity is required, but if you can improvise off of the setup paragraph, no prompt will be able to stump you. I will warn you, however, that improvising a well-thought-out essay can be very hard, even if the examples are given to you. It's much easier to work with examples prepared beforehand.

4. Use personal experience

Let me start off by saying that **you should avoid using personal experience if at all possible.** I've found that students just aren't great at discussing personal experiences in a sophisticated way. The problem is that most personal experiences don't make for intellectually rigorous material. A discussion of your trip to China or how your school's tennis team won the state championships can quickly turn into a mushy story ("I did this ... I did that ... ") that contributes only superficially to your main point. Furthermore, the ACT has released a few sample top scoring essays—none of them use personal experience.

Having said all that, I've seen some high scoring essays that use personal experience to great effect. If you know you're a good writer and English is your best subject, then by all means support your perspective with examples based on personal experience. Otherwise, try coming up with other examples or switch to a logic-based essay (described below).

5. Switch to a logic-based essay

The ACT's top scoring sample essays, both online and in *The Official ACT Prep Guide*, are logic-based essays. As I've discussed in one of the first few chapters, there is nothing wrong with an essay based on logic. It's just not my preferred approach because it doesn't allow for as much preparation. However, it might be the way to go when you're blanking out on a tough prompt. In fact, the template in this book will still work quite nicely for a logic-based essay. The introduction and conclusion would largely stay the same, and you would just have reasoning rather than examples in your first two body paragraphs.

Although I'll show you my own logic-based approach here, I highly recommend you also study the perfect scoring essays the ACT has made available. However, don't put too much stock in them because it's clear the ACT had an agenda when deciding which essays to show. My suspicion is that the essays aren't representative of the best essays they receive.

When writing a logic-based essay, I'll analyze my perspective along two of the following dimensions (these can also help you come up with examples):

- **Economic:** What are the consequences in terms of efficiency, jobs, or the cost of living?
- **Societal:** How do our social interactions, habits, or the way we treat each other change?
- **Cultural:** What is the impact on our values, traditions, and lifestyle?
- **Health:** What are the effects on our health?
- **Innovation:** Does our perspective encourage or hinder creativity and new technology?
- **Environmental:** What are the effects on the environment?
- **Time:** Will we save more time or waste more time? Will we change how we spend our time?
- **Freedom:** Will we have more freedom or less freedom? How does our perspective affect the number of choices we have?

The key is to choose the dimensions that are most applicable to your prompt. Try to write at least one logic-based essay for practice before you actually take the test. It can be a great escape hatch when you're struggling to find relevant examples. And who knows, maybe you'll find that the logic-based approach works better for you than the example-based one.

To show you what a logic-based essay looks like, we'll use the April 2016 essay, which had an extremely tough prompt. The core issue was what society's trend towards casual dress says about our cultural values. Does it reflect the American value of equality (Perspective 1)? Does it show a growing lack of respect for other people and the rules that hold society together (Perspective 2)? Or does it just mean that we value comfort over correctness and that people today care more about who you are, not what you look like (Perspective 3)?

This is exactly the type of prompt for which the logic-based approach may be easier.

Notice that I develop Perspective 3 along economic, time, and cultural lines.

The notion that clothing reflects social status has its roots in historical conventions but its underpinnings are often overlooked. While there are still dress codes for different occasions, casual dress is no longer the affront to social norms that it once was. In fact, many companies today allow employees and even interviewees to show up in casual clothing. Despite all the societal friction the trend towards casual clothing has engendered, it is more in line with modern values of comfort and independence.

Consider the economic implications of a societal dress code. Not only are we forced to purchase different outfits for different social situations but we also waste vast amounts of time hemming and hawing over what to wear. Because the rules are not always clear, we collectively end up spending hours debating the meaning of business casual or whether we can get away with jeans in a "smart casual" event. Furthermore, formal wear is not only uncomfortable but also expensive. Whereas a tee-shirt can be bought for as little as 5 dollars, suits, ties, and dresses can cost hundreds if not thousands of dollars. More and more, people are adopting casual dress as a way of avoiding the frustration and inconvenience of dress codes. Although some may say that casual dress shows a lack of respect for the rules of society, the concept of "correctness" is relative and decided upon through society's values, especially when it comes to clothes. As the costs of "correctness" have become more apparent, our values have shifted towards comfort and convenience, resulting in a wider acceptance of casual dress.

Just as our preference for comfort has grown stronger, so too has our embrace of individual independence, which is also reflected in the trend towards casual dress. Now that the melting pot of America is more diverse than it ever was before, we have become more accustomed to people who talk, act, and dress differently. Not only has the U.S. overseen the immigration of many different groups of people over time, but the ease of travel nowadays has also made it possible for Americans to experience different ways of life in other countries. This exposure to different cultures has taught us to look past people's appearances and appreciate them as individuals. The trend towards casual dress is just a manifestation of our increasing acceptance of diversity. In a society with so many minority groups, it's not only impossible but also frowned upon to enforce one correct way of dressing. Because there is no longer a consensus, the standards of the past are fading, and without fear of judgment, people today are increasingly wearing what they want. While racial conflict is still very much present in America, the progression towards a more inclusive society hasn't stopped, and our clothing preferences reflect that.

Some people assert that the acceptance of casual dress is a reflection of equality, that we view each other as equals. While it's true that fairness and equality are pillars of modern society, these values alone are not enough to fully explain the shifting preferences in what we wear. Indeed, a society in which everyone wears suits can also be considered equal. Our support for equality certainly plays a role in the trend towards casual dress, but it is the economics behind what we wear and our changing demographics that are its true drivers.

In summary, the trend towards casual dress is a reflection of the importance of comfort and our acceptance of diversity. Ultimately, we should all judge people by who they are, not how they look. If we all adopted that attitude, society would be more conductive to progress.

Notice that the body paragraphs do not feature any main examples. There is no extensive background information or storyline. That's the logic-based approach. However, this does not mean you can't use any examples. It simply means that they don't take center stage.

It's also possible to mix the example-based approach with the logic-based one. You could showcase a supporting example in your first paragraph and then make a logical argument in your second. The point is to remain flexible. Don't feel like there's only one way to write the essay. Take the advice in this book and apply it in a way that works best for you and the prompt you're given.

The Essay Should Be Tough

Don't worry if you're feeling overwhelmed. I know this chapter has given you a lot to think about, but the whole process becomes automatic with a little practice. More often than not, your prepared examples will be all you'll need, but even when they don't work out, it should take only 4-5 minutes to think through all the other options during the test.

Some students feel that the example generation process can get quite complicated, but much of it is actually common sense. The reason we have so many backup plans is so that we're fully prepared for any prompt. You can take the ACT only so many times, and you're not always guaranteed an essay assignment that's easy to work with. It sucks to have to take the whole test again just because you weren't prepared for the essay the first time.

I always tell my students to treat the essay as if it were one of the other sections. It should be tough. Just because it's optional and it doesn't factor into the composite score doesn't mean it's not important. If you're applying to top schools, you can bet they'll be using the essay score to evaluate your application. If you take into account all the prep you're doing for the math or English sections, then suddenly it's not unreasonable to go into the essay with 7 to 8 prepared examples. It's not unreasonable to do 10 practice essays. Sometimes that's what it takes to get a perfect score.

Flowchart Summary

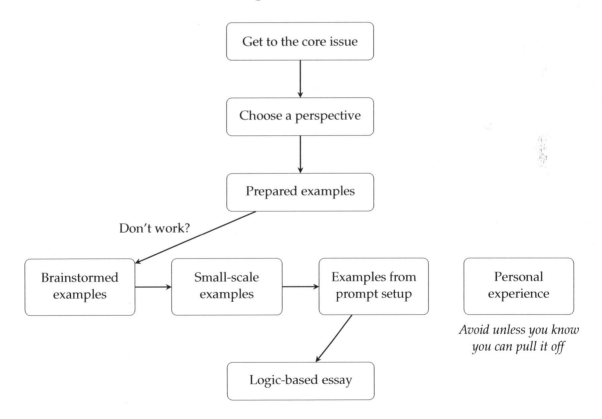

Avoid unless you know you can pull it off

8 Fatal Mistakes Students Make on the Essay

1. Not addressing the core issue

This mistake bears repeating because it's by far the number one mistake, no matter how often students are reminded. The core issue is a guiding force for your essay. It prevents you from straying from the prompt and serves as a good litmus test for the relevance of your examples. Ensure that everything you write plays a role in answering the core issue.

Don't remember how to get to the core issue of a prompt? Go back and reread the one-page chapter.

2. Examples aren't specific enough

Your examples should be well rehearsed with specific events, characters, places, and even dates. The reader should get the impression that you have a complete understanding of what you're writing about. For some reason, I see this mistake come up very often when students write about Apple. Here's a portion from a student essay:

Steve Jobs was a genius. He was insistent on great design and a cool brand image. He worked incredibly hard and never settled on anything less than what he wanted. The iPod and iPhone were revolutionary innovations that changed the world. Apple is now one the leading technological companies in the world, with people eagerly lining up for every new product they launch.

The details above are much too generic and spread-out to say anything meaningful. Just because you own an iPod doesn't mean you're an expert. You should be able to discuss how Steve Jobs treated his employees, the changes his inventions brought to society, how he came up with the iPod, specific instances when he didn't settle on a specific feature, the culture of the Apple stores, etc. Once you understand all the aspects of a topic, then it's easy to pick and choose what you'll focus on for any given prompt.

Your examples should follow the lesson every English teacher repeats—show don't tell. If you want to convey that you're a great violin player, don't just say you're great. That's not persuasive. Tell me how you wake up to Mozart's concertos in the morning. How you sneak off during study hall to practice in the auditorium. How you don't stop practicing until your fingers are bleeding. Ok, maybe that's too graphic, but you get the idea.

3. Examples are too one-dimensional

Another mistake students make is having second examples that say the exact same thing as the first. Although both of your examples should support your argument, you want the second example to add on to your argument rather than repeat it. Think of your examples as layers. The second layer should bring up something new and different that wasn't mentioned in the first layer. Here's a super-short exaggerated example of a one-dimensional essay:

Technology has truly revolutionized our society. For example, Justin Bieber was an unknown recreational singer who started making youtube videos of his songs during his free time. Through the internet, his fanbase started growing and people started to recognize him. A major record label eventually signed him and propelled him into the spotlight. He is now one of the most popular singers among the younger generation. Without technology, he never would've been given the chance he needed.

Similarly, the internet has launched South Korean rapper Psy into international stardom. Prior to his Gangnam Style hit, he was known only throughout Korea. Very few people in the United States and Europe had heard of him. Then when a few celebrities discovered Gangnam Style, they sent messages through social networks like Facebook and Twitter. Within days, the music video went viral and reached millions of viewers. It is only through technology that Psy was able to obtain such a large international fanbase. He is now a global sensation.

Notice how similar the two examples are. Both are about a singer who gained fame through the internet. Though the examples are not bad, it's a little repetitive. It's fine for the first example to be a pop star, but the second should branch out into something else, like how LinkedIn and Facebook are excellent channels for job-seekers looking for new opportunities, or how an excellent education can now be obtained just by watching TED Talks, Khan Academy, and Harvard online courses.

By discussing slightly different examples, you are adding depth and complexity to your argument. You are saying that your argument holds even in different circumstances.

4. Examples aren't related back to your argument

This mistake is a bit different than straying from the core issue. You can have very relevant examples that address the core issue and develop your perspective, but if they aren't related back to your perspective explicitly, the reader may be left wondering how everything ties together. In other words, you should spell out *how* your examples support your perspective. Don't assume readers will make the connection themselves, even when it's obvious. The "While some may argue" and "Without" statements in the template are great opportunities for making the link clear.

5. Your perspective isn't clear

Ah, the essay that doesn't have a perspective—one of the easiest ways to write well and still score poorly. A lot of students like to take the middle road in analyzing all three perspectives, forgetting that the ACT essay requires them to develop a perspective of their own. Your perspective can be in full agreement with any of the others, in partial agreement, or wholly different, but you need to have one. The best way to make sure your essay has a perspective is to write a clear thesis stating your view.

6. Topic Switching

Here's an example of topic switching:

Global warming isn't important because the obesity epidemic is far more damaging. This health issue has led to a decreased quality of life and preventable deaths from conditions such as heart disease and type-2 diabetes. According to recent studies, one-third of all Americans are considered obese. Government funding should be focused on solving this health crisis.

See what happened? An essay that was supposed to be about global warming got warped into one about obesity. Don't abruptly switch topics to force a certain example into your essay. It's obvious to the grader what you're doing.

That being said, there is a line between using something as a supporting example and using it to switch topics. Let's say you wanted to argue against a liberal arts education. In that case, bringing up the need for STEM education would not be a topic switch. Why? Because the two are actually related to one another.

As long as you use common sense when selecting your examples, you'll avoid ever making this mistake.

7. Not writing fast enough

I'm serious about this one. You should be writing like the wind. You should be writing so fast your hand hurts. If you don't believe me, then you haven't tried writing a full 2.5 page essay in 40 minutes.

8. No conclusion

Though missing the conclusion is not as bad as most students think, it's still a glaring error that makes it hard for anyone to ever give you a full score. Always save enough space and enough time for the conclusion. If you miss the conclusion, some graders might not give you the benefit of the doubt—they might just assume you don't know what a conclusion is. A two sentence conclusion is better than no conclusion because at the very least, it shows an understanding of essay organization.

Sample Essays to Official Prompts

This is a sample response to the prompt from the 2015-2016 ACT booklet, which shouldn't be too hard to find with Google. The core issue is whether we should have limits on freedom to protect public health. For instance, can we prohibit smoking to limit the health risks posed to others?

The notion that democracy and individual freedom should be protected at all costs has its roots in the U.S. Constitution and the founding of America but its underpinnings are often overlooked. While we as a society enjoy many rights and freedoms that many outside the U.S. do not, those freedoms have a cost that many of us are blind to. In particular, public health is at risk when we allow anyone to do anything. Despite all the societal friction limiting freedom may engender, we must protect public health even at the cost of certain rights and liberties.

Take, for example, the obesity epidemic in America. Almost one-third of all citizens are now considered obese. How did such a health crisis arise? First, as the digital age has moved our labor force from a physical and active workday to a primarily sedentary one in front of a computer, people have stopped getting the necessary exercise to keep them healthy. Second, and more importantly, big food chains and manufacturers have devised addictive products full of artificial ingredients and sugar. To boost their profits, these companies continue to sell unhealthy products at the expense of the well-being of the American public. One cannot visit an aisle in the grocery store without seeing something packed with high fructose corn syrup, preservatives, or MSG. Because these companies are allowed to sell these detrimental products and advertise them in enticing ways, obesity is now a problem that costs billions of dollars each year, with more and more people suffering from heart disease and Type-2 diabetes. If our government just restricted the type of food products manufacturers could develop and sell, the health of our society would greatly improve. While some may argue that these measures are too extreme, we already have restrictions on alcohol and drug abuse. Some foods are just as dangerous if not more so because although their effects may not be felt in the short term, their repeated consumption will lead to health problems that are just as severe.

In the same way that restrictions would help solve obesity, limitations on automobile use and gas consumption would help solve global warming. Studies now conclude that the Earth is on average 0.9°Celsius warmer than it was during the pre-industrial age. While this increase may seem innocuous, it's enough to induce the melting of the polar ice caps and flood certain coastal areas. Simply put, we cannot continue to emit the same level of carbon dioxide year after year. Cities like Beijing are sometimes covered in smog for weeks at a time due to factory and car pollution. These levels are harmful to the entire population, causing widespread asthma and lung problems. To curb the effect of global warming, restrictions must be placed on our freedom to purchase and drive vehicles that emit a disproportionate amount of harmful pollutants and chemicals. People across the globe should not be able to drive whatever they want and car manufacturers should not be allowed to produce whatever they want. Without such restrictions, pollution will eventually reach alarmingly high levels and our problem of climate change will only get worse.

Still, some proponents of individual freedom point to a fear that once we have too many restrictions, the government will begin to make decisions for us. If laws control what we eat and what we drive, there is little stopping them from controlling what we say and do. However, what these supporters of freedom fail to consider is that the government is made up of people. They don't want to be plagued by the problems of obesity and global warming any more than we do, and they depend on us to be elected. Because interests are aligned, the government overstepping its bounds should be less of a concern. After all, it was the free choices of individuals, not government, that collectively created these problems in the first place. If the government doesn't protect us from ourselves, who will?

As exemplified by the issues of global warming and obesity, we must impose restrictions on actions that would endanger our health. Ultimately, we must give up certain freedoms for our own safety and benefit. If we all adopted that view, society would be more conducive to progress.

This is a sample response to the prompt from Practice Test 1 of *The Official ACT Prep Guide*. The core issue is what the wide availability of free music today says about its value. Has it gone down?

The notion that abundance leads to decreased worth has its roots in economics, but its underpinnings are often overlooked. While music is more accessible than ever before, its value has not declined. In fact, avid listeners today enjoy thousands of songs from bands that simply wouldn't be visible without modern technology. Even with all the societal friction digital technologies have engendered, they have allowed for an increased appreciation of music.

Take, for example, the online, customizable radio service Pandora. By letting Pandora know what type of music you already enjoy, it's able to recommend songs you haven't been exposed to. It then streams those songs and automatically adjusts its recommendations based on positive or negative feedback ("thumbs up" or "thumbs down"). Pandora's immense popularity—it controls 78 percent of Internet radio—is a testament to our desire to constantly find music that we most enjoy. No longer are we limited to the most popular songs on the billboard top 100 list or the selection at the local record store. We can shuffle through Pandora's library of thousands of songs to explore new artists and even new genres. The wide availability of music has only increased our appetite and excitement for music: the next song on the list just might be the catchy tune we play over and over again that week. This enhanced experience and sense of surprise has only encouraged a greater appreciation of music. Although some may say that many Pandora users do not pay for the service, money is not the only indicator of appreciation. The time and attention we give to discovering new music are clear signs of its increasing value.

Just as consumers benefit from Pandora, so too do creators gain notoriety through these free channels. A prime example is Psy, the Korean rapper who created the K-Pop hit "Gangnam Style." Before this hit song, Psy was only known in Korea. Very few people from the U.S. or Europe had heard of him. After all, it's typically the U.S. that exerts its cultural influence on the rest of the world, not the other way around. Within days of the release of "Gangnam Style," however, the music video went viral and spread throughout social media like wildfire. Psy instantly became a global phenomenon and his wacky dance moves were reenacted by everyone who saw them. It was only through channels like YouTube and Facebook, both of which are free, that Psy was able to garner this much attention. People who had never listened to a foreign song in their lives were now singing along in a language they couldn't understand. All of a sudden they became interested in the culture of a country they had previously never bothered to locate on a map. "Gangnam Style" is evidence of the increasing value of music, which has been multiplied by the Internet. Without technology, the discovery and appreciation of foreign music, which enables cross-cultural pollination, would be impossible on a global scale.

Still, detractors of technology assert that the value of music has been diluted by sheer volume. The meaning and significance of each song gets lost when we can simply fast-forward through hundreds of songs at a time. Others say that the availability of other entertainment options has also diminished the value of music. How can music be appreciated when it's being interrupted by text messages and YouTube videos that are accessible all on the same screen? However, what these critics fail to consider is that music plays an integral role in many of these competing options. In fact, most other kinds of entertainment foster an appreciation of music. Movies have soundtracks that later become best-selling albums. Baseball parks play catchy tunes in between innings. And the fact that we can sift through so many songs at once means that we can find the right song to suit our mood. If anything, such a habit is an acknowledgement of music's power in our lives.

As exemplified by Pandora and Psy, we are appreciating music more than ever before. Ultimately, we should all recognize technology as a positive force for music. If we all adopted that view, society would be more conducive to musical innovation.

This is a sample response to the prompt from Practice Test 2 of *The Official ACT Prep Guide*. The core issue is what declining event attendance says about our cultural values in today's society.

The notion that community building requires proximity has its roots in the pre-Internet age but its underpinnings are often overlooked in modern times. While nothing will replace the value of meeting in person, digital technologies have enabled social experiences that rival those that are created face to face. In fact, television and social media have made it possible to build global communities that were previously impossible. Even with all the societal friction meeting online may engender, physical presence simply isn't necessary anymore for building meaningful communities.

Take, for example, the Superbowl, the championship game at the end of each season of American football. While watching the Superbowl live is quite the experience, watching it on television with family and friends has become an event of its own. Even those who aren't fans of the teams that are playing or don't watch football regularly make time to enjoy the experience from the couch. The yearly gathering around the TV has become so popular that a one-minute commercial slot costs upwards of a million dollars. Consequently, spectators are often more interested in the funny commercials than the game itself. Through television, millions of people are able to participate in an event that would otherwise be viewed only by those in the stadium. Just as fans watching live bond with each other by chatting and celebrating together, viewers at home can do the same, strengthening the relationships among friends and family in a shared experience. Although some may say that Superbowl television does not build communities that stretch beyond the living room, the fact that technology now offers more opportunities for social interaction, however small, means that there's less of a need to attend public events for that purpose.

In the same way television can bring people together, social media can allow for more productive presidential debates. Every election year, the major networks hold debates so that the presidential candidates can present their views and weigh the merits of their opponents'. Up until the mass adoption of social media, however, these debates often suffered from questioning that wasn't representative of society's main concerns. After all, the discussion would revolve around questions formulated by potentially biased reporters and not by various members from different demographics. Furthermore, only selected individuals were allowed to participate in the studio audience. Social media fixed this participation problem by making it easy for any user to ask a question through text or video. A sampling of these questions would then be presented to the candidates on stage. Now, citizens from all across the country can participate in an event that was previously off limits to them, and the public can see what issues the country as a whole considers most important. Physical presence is no longer a requirement for participating in civics and policy discussions. Even town hall meetings are taking more and more questions from the Internet. Without social media, we would lose much of the engagement in politics we have today.

Still, some people assert that declining event attendance is not due to television and the Internet but due to convenience and practicality. They believe that time and money have become more important to us than community participation. We'd rather sit on the couch with bag of potato chips than travel for hours to sit in a crowded stadium and eat overpriced hot dogs. While there is some truth to these claims, convenience and cost are only surface reasons for declining event attendance. What many fail to consider is that technology is what enabled the convenience and low cost in the first place. We turn to technology to meet our social needs, and it just so happens that it's cheaper and more convenient. In other words, convenience alone is not enough to explain the lack of participation at public events. It's the enhanced experience through technology that is supplanting the need to go out. If the Internet was eradicated, we'd go back to spending more time and money attending events.

As exemplified by the Superbowl and presidential debates, television and social media offer a shared experience that accounts for the decline in live attendance. Ultimately, we should all come to appreciate the way technology improves our social experiences. If we all adopted that view, society would be more conducive to community building.

This is a sample response to the prompt from Practice Test 3 of *The Official ACT Prep Guide*. The core issue is whether we should have vocational/career training in schools.

The notion that students should receive a well-rounded academic education has its roots in the liberal arts but its underpinnings are often overlooked. While it is important that students have a solid grasp of subjects such as English and math, it is even more important that they are able to become financially productive members of society. In fact, studies have shown that happiness is tied to one's ability to cover the costs of living. Even with all the societal friction instituting vocational programs may engender, they should no doubt be promoted within schools so that students can gain valuable career training.

Take, for example, the current student loan crisis, in which the total debt figure now amounts to over 1.2 trillion dollars. Every year, many students take out hefty loans to go to expensive schools for degrees that likely won't pay off in the future. Not only are they unaware of the financial burden they are placing on themselves but they often have no sense of the career they would like to pursue. This inexperience results in misguided decisions that potentially result in decades of paying back debt. Vocational programs are a solution to this problem. They give students a sense of what's required in the workplace and allow them an opportunity to figure out their strengths and weaknesses, their likes and dislikes. That way, when it comes time to make decisions that will impact their career, they are better prepared to make the right ones for themselves. Although some may say that vocational programs are a waste because it's uncertain what jobs will be available in the future, it's important that students learn who they are in an environment outside traditional schooling, regardless of whether the skills being taught will be relevant in the future.

In the same way that vocational programs can help put a stop to the student loan crisis, they can also close the gender gap in STEM fields. Although women fill close to half of all jobs in the U.S. economy, they hold less than 25 percent of STEM jobs. This is particularly alarming because of the growing shortage of American STEM workers. Many companies cannot find qualified scientists, engineers, and mathematicians to drive innovation and new product development. Many people attribute the gender gap to a cultural issue—girls are expected to be more interested in the humanities than in STEM. Young girls are typically given dolls and jewelry rather than rocket ships and cars. As they get older, this cultural expectation nudges them towards art and theater rather than the math or science team. Soon enough, they begin to lag behind their male peers. If vocational programs were able to promote STEM-related fields early on in schooling, girls would feel more comfortable pursuing them as careers. Increased exposure to science, math, and technology will give them the added confidence they need to become scientists and engineers, and the skills they learn from those vocational classes will give them a head start. If we don't institute vocational programs as an equalizer, the gender gap will persist.

Still, detractors of vocational training assert that schools should only teach academic subjects. They argue that subjects such as history and English develop critical thinking and communication skills that are essential to any job. Vocational programs would distract from the core subjects that empower students to become culturally literate members of society. However, what these critics fail to consider is that cultural literacy oftentimes comes at the cost of financial literacy, hence the cliché "starving artist." While producing more poets and philosophers is certainly a noble goal, our society has reached a point where it's even more of a priority to produce citizens who can contribute to the economy and provide for themselves. Being able to quote Shakespeare is not much of a help when one is living under a mountain of debt. Our economic woes—the gap between the rich and the poor, unemployment, the national debt—can only be solved by putting people to work, and that's what vocational programs do.

As exemplified by the student debt crisis and the gender gap in STEM fields, vocational programs are needed more than ever in schools today. Ultimately, all students should be able to access training that will directly help them make wiser career decisions. If we all adopted that view, society would be more conducive to a healthier economy.

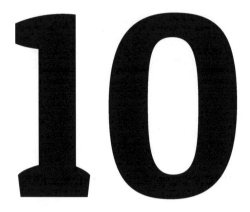

10 High Level Words You Can Use In Any Essay

Although the scripted sentences in the template already contain quite a few high-level words, you'll want to include some of your own in the body paragraphs. Remember that you're graded on vocabulary. It's one of the things graders notice most and one of the easiest ways to impress them.

This chapter lists out 10 high-level words you can use in any essay. I actually don't recommend memorizing all of them. Pick 3-4 that you're comfortable using or come up with your own. Then memorize those words with an acronym. So for my essays, I have *mitigate, detrimental,* and *foster* memorized with the acronym MDF: My Dog Farts. If you go back to my essay in December, you'll notice that I was able to work in *detriment* and *foster*.

1. **mitigate** *(verb)* — to reduce, diminish, lessen, especially pain, damage, or risk

   - Taking time away from technology mitigates much of the damage an attachment to electronic devices may cause.

   - The United Nations is trying to strike a deal that will mitigate the crisis between the two countries.

   - The airline offered free flights to the passengers who lost their bags in order to mitigate any bad publicity.

2. **quintessential** *(adj.)* — to be the perfect example, typical, representative

   - Take, for example, the quintessential app on our phone, facebook.

   - The quintessential argument against technology is that it disconnects us from reality.

3. **superfluous** *(adj.)* — unnecessary

   - Many of the apps we have on our phones are superfluous—they're only there because we downloaded them at some point.

   - Our culture of consumerism results in the superfluous purchases of goods that we don't use.

   - Adding quantum physics to the high school curriculum would be both impractical and superfluous.

4. **detrimental/to someone's detriment** *(adj.)* — harmful/to someone's harm

   - While some may argue that we spend more time with these devices than friends and even family, much to our detriment, actually they connect us to friends and family even more.

   - Allowing cheap imports is detrimental to our economy.

5. **underscore** *(verb)* — to emphasize

   - The rapidly declining population of fish underscores how serious the pollution problem is.

   - The article showed pictures of car crashes to underscore the dangers of drunk driving.

6. **undermine** *(verb)* — to weaken or damage

   - Opponents have been showing attack ads in the state to undermine John's campaign for the presidency.

   - Our addiction to electronic devices undermines our ability to focus for long periods of time.

7. **foster** *(verb)* — to encourage, to promote, to support

   - The widespread availability of books, music, and products fosters the spread of ideas and promotes the work of artists and writers who may have been invisible otherwise.

   - Government subsidies have fostered the growth of the farming industry.

8. **juxtapose** *(verb)* — to place side by side for the purposes of contrast

   - When we juxtapose the benefits with the drawbacks, it's easy to see that the value of technology far outweighs its costs.

   - The juxtaposition of the salaries of CEOs and those of regular workers reflects the ever increasing gap between the rich and the poor.

9. **exacerbate** *(verb)* — to make worse

   - The more devices we own, the more we exacerbate our disconnect from the real world.

   - The disagreement over global warming has only exacerbated the concerns about the environment.

10. **supplant** *(verb)* — to replace

    - Those who are in favor of limiting technology use suggest that we supplant our digital activities with physical ones—sports, reading, and meeting friends in person.

    - Even though online courses are becoming popular, there is nothing that can supplant a teacher's presence in a classroom.

    - This new television will supplant last year's model.

11

5 Essay Prompts for Practice

Safety and Privacy

In an age when technology and social media allow others to peer more deeply into our lives than ever before, the conflict between the right to privacy and the need for safety has intensified. For example, government surveillance captures our text messages and phone calls in order to obtain information to thwart terrorist attacks. Security cameras in school deter and solve crime but may not promote a comfortable environment for students to express themselves. What is lost when we limit privacy for security and what is gained? Given the constantly changing dynamic between privacy and safety in our digital world, it is worth considering whether one should be sacrificed for the other.

Read and consider these perspectives. Each suggests a particular way of thinking about the conflict between safety and privacy.

Perspective One	Perspective Two	Perspective Three
Government cannot keep us safe without relevant information. Privacy must sometimes be given up so that law enforcement has the resources necessary to protect us.	Privacy should be limited so that we live in a more transparent society. An increased awareness of those around us helps us make safer decisions.	What could keep society more safe than privacy itself? When personal information can easily be obtained, public safety is compromised.

Essay Task

Write a unified, coherent essay in which you evaluate multiple perspectives on the conflict between safety and privacy. In your essay, be sure to:
- analyze and evaluate the perspectives given
- state and develop your own perspective on the issue
- explain the relationship between your perspective and those given

Your perspective may be in full agreement with any of the others, in partial agreement, or wholly different. Whatever the case, support your ideas with logical reasoning and detailed, persuasive examples.

Sports in Schools
Based on the Official February 2016 Prompt

In our schools, academics is often followed by athletics. Not only do we have physical education classes that allow us to participate in sports but almost all schools make sports activities available to students once classes are over. But as sports continues to get promoted within schools, the increasing concern is that athletics is becoming more important to students than academics. Students who compete in team sports are often required to spend so much time in practice that they have little time left for homework afterwards. Competition among rival teams can pressure students into taking even more time and energy away from their studies. As it becomes harder and harder to maintain a healthy balance between sports and academics, it is important that we examine whether sports should continue to be promoted within schools.

Read and consider these perspectives. Each suggests a particular way of thinking about the presence of sports in schools.

Perspective One	**Perspective Two**	**Perspective Three**
Sports activities should be promoted in schools. They develop a sense of community by bonding people through a common interest.	School should be about academics. Sports distracts the focus of students away from their studies.	Sports teaches important lessons that school cannot—teamwork, leadership, overcoming adversity. If sports weren't allowed in schools, students wouldn't be able to learn these life skills.

Essay Task

Write a unified, coherent essay in which you evaluate multiple perspectives on the conflict between safety and privacy. In your essay, be sure to:

- analyze and evaluate the perspectives given
- state and develop your own perspective on the issue
- explain the relationship between your perspective and those given

Your perspective may be in full agreement with any of the others, in partial agreement, or wholly different. Whatever the case, support your ideas with logical reasoning and detailed, persuasive examples.

Mandatory Community Service

Though community service is available at many schools in the country, only some of them require a certain number of hours for graduation. These schools claim that community service helps students become better people while improving the local community at the same time. They believe that that the value of community service can sometimes only be seen in hindsight and if it weren't mandatory, students would simply miss out on the opportunity. Others, however, see it as a burden. They argue that if made mandatory, community service becomes just another box a student must check to graduate. Given the sheer number of schools that allow students to participate in community service, it is important that we examine whether community service should be made mandatory for graduation.

Read and consider these perspectives. Each suggests a particular way of thinking about whether community service should be mandatory for graduation.

Perspective One	**Perspective Two**	**Perspective Three**
Community service exposes students to new people, situations, and problems. By helping others, they gain a broader perspective on the world and an increased sense of responsibility.	Students today already have too much to do. Mandatory community service hours would only overwhelm them even more.	Community service should be a choice. It loses its purpose if students are forced to do it.

Essay Task

Write a unified, coherent essay in which you evaluate multiple perspectives on the conflict between safety and privacy. In your essay, be sure to:
- analyze and evaluate the perspectives given
- state and develop your own perspective on the issue
- explain the relationship between your perspective and those given

Your perspective may be in full agreement with any of the others, in partial agreement, or wholly different. Whatever the case, support your ideas with logical reasoning and detailed, persuasive examples.

Competition in the Learning Process

Students today face a never-ending stream of competitions—school club positions, sports, college admissions. The pressure to compete is at every turn. The question, then, is whether competition is healthy for them. Some researchers indicate that it prepares students to excel in today's fast-paced and highly competitive world where we compete for jobs and houses. Others say that a winner-take-all mentality can easily damage one's self-esteem and lead to resentment. The result is that students are discouraged from activities they may otherwise enjoy. Given the competitive world we live in, it is important that we examine whether competition is beneficial in the learning process.

Read and consider these perspectives. Each suggests a particular way of thinking about whether competition is healthy for student development.

Perspective One	Perspective Two	Perspective Three
Competition inspires students to do their best. Through immediate feedback, they learn to grow and improve themselves in challenging situations.	Competition teaches students to accept failure without losing self esteem. Without it, they wouldn't learn how to handle disappointment.	Competition makes winning the sole objective. It creates a negative environment that inhibits learning and cooperation.

Essay Task

Write a unified, coherent essay in which you evaluate multiple perspectives on the conflict between safety and privacy. In your essay, be sure to:
- analyze and evaluate the perspectives given
- state and develop your own perspective on the issue
- explain the relationship between your perspective and those given

Your perspective may be in full agreement with any of the others, in partial agreement, or wholly different. Whatever the case, support your ideas with logical reasoning and detailed, persuasive examples.

Patriotism

Even in today's global society, patriotism—pride in one's country—thrives almost everywhere. Athletes at the World Cup and at the Olympics proudly wave their flags in support of their homeland. Those who serve in their country's military are held in high honor and esteem. In America, many bumper stickers can be seen touting American values. Although patriotism is alive and well, many question its value in our modern world. Some see it as an excuse for arrogance and egotism, for one country to disparage another. Others say unity and solidarity are necessary for any nation to make progress. Given how connected we are to people from other countries, some thought should be given to whether patriotism still has a place in our modern world.

Read and consider these perspectives. Each suggests a particular way of thinking about whether patriotism is beneficial in today's global society.

Perspective One	Perspective Two	Perspective Three
Pride in one's country is what unites members of a society. When citizens come together, they're able to accomplish more.	Patriotism undermines diversity and understanding. It breeds resentment and encourages prejudices against people from other countries.	Patriotism compels people to blindly defend the actions and policies of their own government. When their country makes a mistake, many are unwilling to acknowledge it.

Essay Task

Write a unified, coherent essay in which you evaluate multiple perspectives on the conflict between safety and privacy. In your essay, be sure to:
- analyze and evaluate the perspectives given
- state and develop your own perspective on the issue
- explain the relationship between your perspective and those given

Your perspective may be in full agreement with any of the others, in partial agreement, or wholly different. Whatever the case, support your ideas with logical reasoning and detailed, persuasive examples.

12
Appendix A

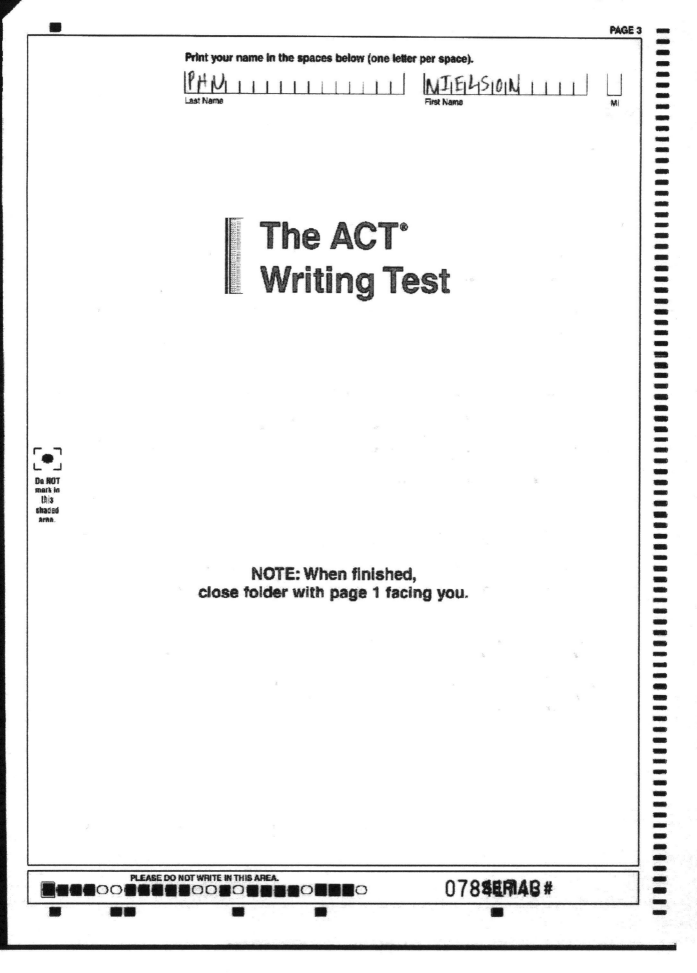

Please enter the
information at the
right before beginning
the Writing Test.

Use a soft lead No. 2
pencil only. Do NOT
use a mechanical
pencil, ink, ballpoint, or
felt-tip pen.

WRITING TEST BOOKLET NUMBER
Print your 6-digit
Booklet Number
in the boxes at the
right.

2 5 9 8 9 0

WRITING TEST FORM

2 2 N

Print your
3-character
Test Form in
the boxes above
and fill in the
corresponding
oval at the right.

○ 22A   ○ 22R   ○ 23H   ○ 89D
○ 22C   ○ 22T   ○ 23K   ○ 89F
○ 22E   ○ 22U   ○ 24A   ○ 89G
○ 22G   ○ 22W   ○ 24C   ○ 89H
○ 22J   ○ 22Y   ○ 24E   ○ 89J
○ 22L   ○ 23B   ○ 24G   ○ 89K
● 22N   ○ 23D   ○ 24J   ○ 89L
○ 22P   ○ 23F   ○ 24L   ○ 89N

Begin WRITING TEST here.

The notion that technology will doom mankind has its roots in ominous sci-fi movies and novels but the underpinnings are often overlooked. While it is true that modern society is becoming increasingly dependent on devices such as cell phones, this dependency should not be frowned upon. In fact, many of technology's capabilities allow us to experience the world in ways we never could've imagined. Even with all the societal friction technological devices may engender, the benefits outweigh the costs and we should embrace our digital world, not fight it.

Take, for example, the many applications available on cell phones today. These "apps", such as facebook, Uber, and airbnb connect us in ways that were previously impossible. Facebook allows us to chat with friends and family halfway across the world. Uber connects drivers looking for part-time income with daily commuters at the click of a button. Airbnb allows homeowners who have an empty room to profit from a tourist or visitor who prefers a more local experience than that of a hotel, which is often more expensive. In fact, airbnb found places to stay for more than 50,000 visitors in Brazil during the 2014 World Cup. Furthermore, in times of emergency, it is these very "apps" that get criticized for disconnecting us from reality that provide updates and the

If you need more space, please continue on the next page.

IM-194997-001:864321

Do not write in this shaded area.

WRITING TEST

locations of safe havens. While some may argue that we spend more time with these devices than friends and even family, much to our detriment, actually they connect us to friends and family even more. We should welcome this enhanced connection instead of avoiding it.

In the same way that cell phones open up new ways for society to connect, companies are ushering in new possibilities through technology and our devices. Amazon, the online retail site, now makes it easy to order everything from books to mattresses from the comfort of one's home. No longer are we confined to the limited selection at the local bookstore. This widespread availability of books, music, and products fosters the spread of ideas and promotes the work of artists and writers who may not have been noticed otherwise. Writers like Amanda Hocking and others have self-published their work to great success. In addition to Amazon, search engines like Google open up a world of information not limited by the scope of an encyclopedia. By democratizing information and enabling users to share it, these sites serve as portals of connection, not isolation. Without technology and the devices we use, we would be stripped of the enrichment that websites like Amazon and Google could provide.

Still, technology's detractors assert that our dependency stifles our relationships with those in our presence. After all, who doesn't have a friend who's seemingly addicted to texting and online shopping? What these critics fail to consider is that there is more communication now than ever before and to remove oneself from the digital world is to experience the very

WRITING TEST

solitary condition they detest. Indeed, much of society has already embraced the benefits of technology and there is very little that can turn us back. Many families have already disconnected their land lines in favor of cell phones. Many malls and retail stores have closed, failing to compete with their online rivals, for better or worse. Many books are now being read on "e-readers" such as the Kindle or Nook. Our cars today come equipped with GPS, and many would feel lost without them. The world has already embraced these devices and our dependency should not be resisted.

As exemplified by many cell phone apps such as airbnb and sites like Amazon and Google, the benefits of digital devices outweigh the costs, and in fact, open up more avenues for human connection. Ultimately we should not take up arms against technology but welcome it. If we all adopted that view, our society would be more conducive to innovation and progress.

Made in the USA
San Bernardino, CA
16 May 2018